HEROES ON HORSEBACK:

THE PONY EXPRESS

Steven Otfinoski

GReaT S♣uRCe®
EDUCATION GROUP
A Division of Houghton Mifflin Company

Reading Advantage Authors

Laura Robb
James F. Baumann
Carol J. Fuhler
Joan Kindig

Project Manager

Ellen Sternhell

Editor

Jeri Cipriano

Design and Production

Preface, Inc.

Photography and Illustration

All cover, interior art by Chris Ellison, except for the following: pp. 6, 33, 57, 60 © Bettmann/Corbis; p. 20 map art by Sue Carlson; p. 26 © Phil Schermeister/Corbis; pp. 41t, 48 © St. Joseph Museum Inc., St. Joseph, Missouri; p. 41b © Corbis; p. 51 © The Granger Collection; p. 58 © Craig Aurness/Corbis; p. 62 © Wolfgang Kaehler/Corbis

Printed in the United States of America

International Standard Book Number: 0-669-51405-5

2 3 4 5 6 7 8 9 10 - RRDC - 09 08 07 06 05

CONTENTS

CHAPTER

1

The First Ride

The young rider on the small horse smiled at the excited crowd of people gathered around him. He looked up at the bright banners and flags that hung from the Patee House, the finest hotel in St. Joseph, Missouri. Nearby, a brass band was playing a lively tune. A small group of distinguished-looking gentlemen stood in front of the hotel. One of them was making a speech to the crowd. But it was not the speaker or the band the crowd had come to see. It was the rider and his horse.

The pony whinnied and pawed the ground. It didn't like people pulling hair from its mane and tail. Some people wanted a strand of its hair as a souvenir of this historic occasion. The rider didn't tell them to stop because he knew it wouldn't hurt the horse. He, too, knew how special this day was.

The young rider looked up nervously at the big clock in the street. He worried about the delay, but he tried not to show it.

Then, a man brought welcome news. The train had finally arrived with the mail the rider was waiting for. The mail was delivered to the post office. Shortly afterwards, someone shot off a cannon. Responding to the signal, rider and horse raced up the street to the post office. The anxious crowd followed quickly behind. This was the moment they had all been waiting for.

At the post office, the postmaster came out carrying a strange-looking saddlebag. The saddlebag held forty-nine letters, five telegrams, and a few newspapers from back East. One of the telegrams was from the president of the United States, James Buchanan. The postmaster handed the saddlebag to the rider, who put it over the horn of his saddle.

As the crowd cheered him on, the rider made his way down to the ferry dock. He walked his horse onto the steamboat *Denver*. The steamboat whistle blew sharply. Then, the large boat slipped away from the shore and into the dark waters of the Missouri River. A short time later, the boat reached the opposite shore of Elwood, Kansas. It was here that the rider's journey would really begin. He gave the reins a tug and the horse trotted off the boat and into the night.

People cheered the Pony Express rider, welcoming him and the arrival of their mail.

Soon, both rider and horse were lost from sight in the gathering darkness. The date was April 3, 1860, and the Pony Express was off and running.

How It All Began

No one is sure who that first Pony Express rider was. Some say he was Bill Richardson. Others say he was Johnny Fry. Still, others think it was Jack Keetley, who rode the first leg of the long journey from St. Joseph, Missouri, to Sacramento, California.

We do know, however, the man who made the speech to the crowd. He was Alexander Majors, one of the three businessmen whose company had started the Pony Express.

The story of how the Pony Express came to be is an interesting one. It really began when gold was discovered in Sacramento Valley, California, in 1848. Tens of thousands of Americans rushed to California's gold fields to strike it rich. Few of them became rich, but many decided to stay anyway.

California had a sunny climate, lots of land, and rich soil for growing crops. Within two short years, California's population grew from under fifteen thousand to one hundred thousand. That was enough people to make California a state in 1850.

California saw great changes in the next ten years. Mining camps became towns. Towns became cities. But one thing didn't change—the mail service. It was as slow as ever.

The stagecoach run by the Butterfield Company took twenty-three days to reach California from St. Joseph, Missouri, where the country's railroad line ended. Californians didn't like this. They wanted to get letters from their families and friends back East more quickly. They also wanted to get the news of what was happening in the East. Northern and Southern states were growing further apart over the issue of Southern slavery. Some people said there might be a war.

California Senator William Gwin wanted to do something to improve the mail service. In late 1859, he met with William H. Russell, one of Alexander Majors's business partners in a company that transported freight, or goods. (That was the Central Overland and Pikes Peak Express Company.) The two men decided that a lone rider could carry the mail west much faster than the stagecoach. The rider would ride until his horse was tired. Then, he would mount a fresh horse at a relay station.

William H. Russell ran a Western freight service when he founded the Pony Express in 1860.

When the rider became tired, a fresh rider would replace him. A string of riders, Russell believed, could cover the 1,966 miles (3,164 kilometers) from St. Joseph to Sacramento, California, in ten days. That was less than half the time it took the stagecoach to make the trip. Russell and Gwin called the mail service the "horse express." Soon, people were calling it the Pony Express.

After the meeting, Russell rushed back to his home office in Kansas. There, he told his two partners about his plan. Neither Alexander Majors nor the other partner, William Waddell, liked the idea of the Pony Express. They felt it would cost too much and would never make a profit. Russell argued that if they could make the Pony Express a success, the government would give them a contract to continue the service. Then, they would make up any money they had spent on setting up the business. He convinced his two partners to back the idea of a Pony Express.

Up and Running

There was much work to do. Russell had promised Senator Gwin he would have the Pony Express up and running in just a few short months.

The first Pony Express rider to arrive in Sacramento
was greeted with great joy.

Horses had to be bought and riders hired. Stations had to be set up along the trail so riders could change horses and rest.

Would it work? Nine days and twenty-three hours after that first unknown rider left St. Joseph, another Pony Express rider rode into Sacramento with the mail. He had beaten the ten-day goal by one hour!

People were so happy to see the rider that they crowded around him. A young woman ran up to the rider's horse and tied her bonnet on its head. The crowd laughed and cheered. A band played the song "See the Conquering Hero Comes." To the people of California, the Pony Express rider was a true hero, a hero on horseback. The first run of the Pony Express had been a huge success.

2

Brave Men, Hardy Horses

Who were these heroes on horseback, the bold riders of the Pony Express?

Russell and his partners wanted their riders to have four important qualifications. First, they had to be young and strong. They would need to endure long days and nights on the trail. Second, they had to be excellent horsemen who could ride with skill and speed. Third, they had to know every inch of the territory they were to ride through. Finally, they had to be lightweight, weighing no more than one hundred twenty pounds. The Pony Express was built on speed. If the riders were too heavy, they would slow down and tire out the horses they rode.

There was one more qualification applicants had to meet. Every rider had to take a serious oath. Each promised not to use bad language, drink liquor, or fight with other company workers.

Riders also vowed to be faithful to their duty and honest at all times. They promised to treat their horses and other company animals kindly. If chased by Indians, they promised not to shoot unless shot at first. Violence was to be used only as a last resort in self-defense.

Here is one of the advertisements that Russell's company ran in newspapers throughout the West.

The Men

The pay must have impressed the young men who read the ads in the newspapers. One hundred dollars a month was more money than any of them had ever earned before. The part about risking death daily didn't scare them off. Their lives on farms and in towns were boring and ordinary. They longed for the kind of adventures they would have as Pony Express riders. They also yearned for glory and fame.

As soon as it started, the Pony Express captured the imagination of the nation. Everyone looked at Express riders with respect and admiration. Young girls adored them. No young man minded that!

Hundreds of young men applied for a job as a Pony Express rider. Only the best eighty men were chosen. The age limit in the ad was misleading. The average age of riders hired was twenty-two, although some riders were as young as fourteen years old.

Those men who weren't selected at first remained hopeful. Few riders stayed with the Pony Express for long. Many didn't last longer than a year. The work was hard and the hours long. Because of this, replacements were always needed.

Some new riders came from men who were doing other work for the company. These included station workers, freight carriers, messengers, and stock tenders who cared for the animals.

The Horses

Pony Express horses were as carefully chosen as the riders. They had to be small and fast. The maximum height for a horse was fifty-nine inches. (That's just under five feet in height.) The horses weighed an average of nine hundred pounds. They were called "ponies" because of their small size, not their age. Most of them were full-grown horses.

Some of the horses were bought from horse breeders. Many more were wild mustangs from the open plains. Cowboys rounded up these horses. Then, professional horse trainers "broke" them so they wouldn't throw their riders. But the trainers didn't break the horses' spirits. According to station keeper Peter Neece, a horse was considered trained "when a rider could lead it out of the stable without getting his head kicked off."

The Pony Express used four hundred to five hundred horses. Many of them were wild mustangs caught in the West.

Pony Express horses were well cared for. They were fed only grain to make them strong. Indian horses were fed mostly grass, which was less nutritious. Because of this, the Pony Express horses were stronger and faster than Indian horses. Riders' lives were saved many times by their horses being able to outrun attacking Indians.

The Pony Express horses were intelligent, too. If a rider was killed along the route, his horse continued on to the next station with the mail. If the riders earned their salaries, their horses surely earned their grain—and then some!

CHAPTER
3
On the Trail

The Pony Express route was basically the old Oregon Trail. This was the trail that many pioneers followed west in the 1840s. It cut across eight present-day states. From St. Joseph, Missouri, the trail went south into Kansas. Then it curved north across the grasslands of southwestern Nebraska and dipped into Colorado territory and entered Wyoming. There the trail became more rugged and rocky.

From Wyoming, the trail went into northern Utah and Salt Lake City. This was one of the few cities the trail passed through. After going around the Great Salt Lake, the trail entered a vast, barren region. People called it the Great American Desert. This desert area was hot with little water. Desert dust storms could choke the rider and horse.

Alkali, a white mineral salt, covered the parched ground like snow. When the horses stirred up the ground, the alkali went into the air. It burned the throat and eyes of the horses and the riders.

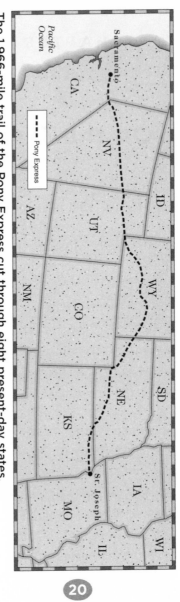

The 1,966-mile trail of the Pony Express cut through eight present-day states.

But there was worse to come. The trail from Nevada into California crossed through the towering Sierra Nevada Mountains. Riders had to pass through narrow, rocky mountain passes. In winter, these passes were filled with deep snowdrifts. In spring, they might be flooded with melted snow.

The normal pace for riders in deserts and plains averaged one hundred twenty miles per day. It often dropped to only fifty-five miles per day in the Sierra Nevadas. Once over the mountains, the trail led down into Sacramento, California. From there, mail for San Francisco, the last stop, was delivered by boat down the Sacramento River.

Two Kinds of Stations

The Pony Express set up stations to provide fresh horses and a place for riders to exchange the mail. The first stations were set up fifty to one hundred miles apart. But the company discovered that this was too far for the horses to travel. So, more stations were added in between. In the end, there were one hundred ninety stations along the Pony Express trail. They had colorful names like Warm Creek, Big Sandy, and Devil's Gate.

The exchange of the mail between riders was made in two minutes or less.

There were two kinds of stations. Relay stations were small. They were often no more than a wooden shack, a cave, or a tent. A corral, a fenced-in area, was out back for the horses. These stations were meant to serve simply as places for pony riders to switch horses.

Home stations, set about seventy-five miles apart, were larger. Many home stations were old stagecoach stops. It was here where the riders rested between runs. They ate meals and slept in bunks. There might be as many as six or more workers at the home station. There was a station keeper and several stock tenders. The stock tenders cared for the horses and other animals. Workers were usually men, but some station keepers were women.

Each Pony Express rider was responsible for about a seventy-five-mile section of the route. His workday began at his home station. He would wait anxiously for the sound of pounding hooves. This was the signal that a rider was approaching.

Carrying the Mail

As soon as the rider arrived, he leaped off his horse. He transferred his leather saddlebag, called a *mochila* (moh KEE lah), to a fresh horse. This saddlebag had a hole in the front so it could easily be slipped over the saddle. The rider's weight kept it securely in place. Four locked, leather boxes were attached to the four corners of the mochila. Inside these boxes called *cantinas* was the mail.

Letters were written on tissue-thin paper and wrapped up in oiled silk. This protected them from the harsh weather conditions. The writing paper was thin to keep down the weight. Pony Express prices were high. It cost $5 to send a half-ounce letter to Sacramento. In time, the price dropped to about $1 per half ounce.

The new rider jumped onto his horse and took off. The whole process took less than two minutes. There was barely a moment to exchange more than a few words with the station keeper or the other rider. The rider rode for ten to fifteen miles before reaching his first relay station. There, he would quickly change horses and be on his way again.

On an average run, a rider might stop and change horses five to seven times before arriving at the next home station. There, he would turn over the mochila to the next rider. The weary rider could then settle down for a hot meal prepared by the station keeper, some conversation, and maybe a good night's sleep in a bunk bed.

Mochila is Spanish for "purse." This leather saddlebag contained the all-important mail.

After a meal and a night's rest, the rider would then be ready to greet a new rider—this time, one heading east with mail from California. After all, the Pony Express ran in both directions. The rider would take the mochila filled with Sacramento's mail and start back on the same route he had taken the day before. He wouldn't rest again until he had arrived back at his own home station. All tired out, he would get some rest before starting the process all over again.

It's no wonder most Pony Express riders "burned out" in a matter of months. It was hard work!

4

Wild Bill Hickok

The life of a Pony Express rider was often filled with danger. But station keepers often found themselves in even greater danger. Many stations were in remote, faraway places. This made them vulnerable, or open, to attacks from outlaws or Indians.

One of the most celebrated station workers was James Butler Hickok, later known as "Wild Bill." When he first came to work for the Pony Express, Hickok was in his early twenties. He was too big to be a Pony Express rider, so the company put him to work as a wagon master. While on the job, Hickok was attacked by a grizzly bear. The bear tore his scalp, clawed his left arm, and badly bruised the rest of his body before Hickok could kill it with a knife and pistol.

The company sent Hickok home to Kansas to recuperate. When he was feeling better, they gave him light work at the Rock Creek Station in southeastern Nebraska. Hickok's job was to water and feed the horses and livestock.

Grizzly bears were common in the West at the time
that Hickok was attacked. The attack happened
while he was leading a wagon train carrying supplies.

The Rock Creek Station

A man named David McCanles had owned the Rock Creek Station property. He was a rich rancher and a known bully. McCanles ran the nearby town as if it were his personal property. He didn't like James Hickok from the first time he saw him. McCanles would visit the station and call Hickok names like Duck Bill, making fun of his large upper lip. McCanles would sometimes push Hickok around, even though the young man was still healing from his wounds.

When McCanles sold his property to the Pony Express, the company wasn't able to pay him right away due to financial problems. McCanles complained to the station keeper, Horace Wellman. Wellman told McCanles that there was nothing he could do and that he would just have to wait. That only made McCanles angrier.

On July 12, 1861, McCanles arrived at the station early in the afternoon. He told Wellman that he wanted his money. The station keeper explained that headquarters told him the day before that they still couldn't pay McCanles. That's when the rancher said he was taking back his property and ordered Wellman to get out. Wellman refused. McCanles said that he would be back, and he left.

McCanles returned a few hours later, wearing a gun. This time he wasn't alone. Riding with him were his cousin and one of his ranch hands. McCanles had also brought along his twelve-year-old son. He told the others to wait for him while he went to the station house.

Wellman wouldn't come out to meet the rancher. James Hickok went to the door instead. McCanles taunted the younger man and told him to come outside and fight like a man. But Hickok wasn't about to take any more of McCanles's bullying. He drew his gun inside the station. McCanles came through the door. Hickok fired at him through a curtain. McCanles stumbled out into the yard and fell, a bullet through his heart.

His two companions came running at the sound of the shot. Hickok took aim and shot one of the men, wounding him. The other one ran, but Hickok fired and wounded him, too.

Hickok had had enough of shooting, so he put his gun away. But Wellman and another station hand were angry. They finished off the two wounded men. They would have killed McCanles's son, too, if Hickok hadn't stopped them. The boy fled for his life.

David McCanles had pushed Hickok too far, and he paid for it with his life.

Three days later Hickok, Wellman, and the other station hand were arrested and charged with murder. They claimed they had killed in self-defense while defending government property. The charges were quickly dismissed.

Gun Fighter and Law Officer

Soon after the charges were dismissed, James Hickok left the Pony Express. He would begin his career as a gunfighter and for a time would serve as a law officer. His quick draw and courage would earn him the name "Wild Bill" Hickok.

Wild Bill Hickok became one of the most feared gunfighters in the West.

CHAPTER

5

Buffalo Bill

Another man who started with the Pony Express and became a Western legend was William F. Cody. He is better known as Buffalo Bill. Cody came to work for the Pony Express when he was only eleven years old.

Cody grew up in Kansas, where his father was an abolitionist, a person who is against slavery. Cody's father died as a result of stab wounds he suffered at the hands of pro-slavers. Cody was very young when his father died. But he had to go to work to support his mother and three sisters.

The company hired Cody to be a messenger between wagon trains carrying goods westward. The young man did his job well, but he wanted more adventure. He applied for a job as a Pony Express rider.

Alexander Majors gave him a short route of about forty-five miles in Colorado to test his abilities. Cody passed the test and worked the same route for two months. In the summer of

1860, he left the Pony Express and went home to see his ill mother in Kansas.

While back in Kansas, Cody met William Russell. This time, he asked Russell to hire him for another Pony Express route. Russell sent him to see Joseph Slade. Slade was in charge of several stations in Wyoming. Slade thought Cody was too young and inexperienced to be a regular rider. But he finally agreed to give him a chance. He gave Cody a difficult seventy-six-mile route along the North Platte River.

A Tough Rider

Cody made it through his ride and arrived at his home station. There, he learned that his relief rider had been killed the night before in a fight.

The station keeper asked Cody to make the next leg of the trip. He agreed. So Cody rode another eighty-five miles to Red Buttes. By the time he returned to his starting point, Cody had traveled 322 miles. It was the third-longest ride in Pony Express history.

A week later, Cody was riding the same route when he came upon a band of Sioux Indians. They began to chase him. Cody urged his pony on. He lay flat against the horse's back as it galloped onward. Soon, the band of Sioux was left far behind.

Cody was an excellent rider. It didn't matter whether he was lying flat on his horse's back or hunched forward in a gallop.

When Cody arrived at the Sweetwater Station, he was in for a shock. Indians had killed the stock tender and driven off all the horses. Cody brought the tragic news to the next station on his route.

A Narrow Escape

Cody continued to work for the Pony Express as a part-time rider. This gave him time for his favorite pastime, hunting.

One day he was hunting for bear, but all he caught were a couple of sage hens. Night came and Cody stopped to set up camp.

Cody heard a horse whinny nearby and went to investigate. He was carrying his rifle and the two dead birds. He came upon a cabin and could hear men's voices inside. He entered the cabin and came face to face with eight men. He recognized two of them from his days on the wagon train. They had been fired under suspicion of robbing and murdering a rancher. Cody realized that he was in the midst of a violent gang.

The two men didn't recognize Cody, but he still knew his life was in danger. Cody said he would go back to fetch his horse. Two of the men insisted they go with him. Cody left his rifle in the cabin, but he still had his two pistols.

As they walked back down the trail, Cody knew he had to escape or risk being killed. On purpose, he stopped and dropped one of the dead hens he was carrying. When one of the men bent over to pick it up, Cody struck him over the head with the butt of a pistol. The other man went for his gun and Cody shot him. The man crumpled to the ground.

Cody could hear noises from the cabin above. He knew the others would soon be coming after him. He ran for his horse and rode off. Soon he could hear the pounding hoofbeats of the gang's horses. It would be only a matter of minutes before they were upon him.

Cody stopped and slipped off his horse. He slapped the horse's flank and it continued on. Then he hid behind some rocks. He held his breath as the men approached on horseback. They went right past him, thinking he was still on his horse.

Cody walked the twenty-five miles back to the nearest Pony Express station. He arrived tired and footsore. He told the station keeper what had happened. The station keeper and a posse of men chased after the outlaw gang.

Young Cody's quick thinking saved him from being captured and killed by the outlaws.

Cody led the posse to the cabin, but the outlaws were gone. Near the cabin, they found a freshly dug grave. It was where the men had buried the man Cody had shot in self-defense.

Hunter, Scout, Showman

Cody remained with the Pony Express until June 1861. Then he felt homesick and went back to Kansas to visit his family. He later became a scout for the U.S. Army in Indian territory. After that, he worked as a buffalo hunter for the railroad. He provided the railroad workers with fresh meat. This job earned him the name "Buffalo Bill."

Years later, Buffalo Bill became a showman. He produced and starred in a Wild West show that traveled all across the country. One of the show's highlights was a Pony Express rider changing horses. Cody never forgot his days as a Pony Express rider. He did more than any other person to keep its memory alive.

William F. Cody at about age fourteen, when he rode for the Pony Express

William F. Cody in his forties, when he ran his Wild West show

CHAPTER
6
Pony Bob

The most respected Pony Express rider is not as well-known today as Wild Bill Hickok or Buffalo Bill. He was Robert Haslam, better known as "Pony Bob."

Haslam was born in London, England. He came to the United States as a teenager. He was hired by the Pony Express to build relay stations. Later, he became a rider. His route ran from Friday's Station at the foot of Lake Tahoe east to Bucklands Station, Nevada.

The Paiute Indians lived in this region. They were angry with the white settlers who were stealing their land and killing their people. They finally decided to fight back. On May 7, 1860, a band of young Paiute warriors attacked the Williams Station in Nevada and killed five men.

Over the next two months, other stations were attacked and burned. Every time a Pony Express rider headed out with the mail, he didn't know if he would make it to the next station alive.

But this didn't stop Pony Bob. He believed in the Pony Express motto, "The mail must go through!" Two days after the Williams Station tragedy, Bob arrived at a relay station to find no fresh horses. Men had taken them all to go fight the Paiutes. Bob fed his horse and rode on to his last stop, his home station in Bucklands.

His relief rider, Johnson Richardson, refused to take the mochila and do his run. He said it was too dangerous to ride as long as there was fighting going on. The station keeper turned to Pony Bob in desperation. He offered him a fifty-dollar bonus if he would take Richardson's run. It took Haslam only moments to say yes. Ten minutes later, he was off on a fresh horse on another seventy-five-mile run.

When he finally arrived at Smith's Creek Station, Pony Bob had traveled a total of 190 miles. After several hours' rest, he was back in the saddle again. He carried the westbound mail across the same route he had earlier traveled east.

Pony Bob lived by the motto, "The mail must go through!"

The Longest Ride

When Pony Bob arrived back at Cold Creek Station, he found a terrible sight. The station keeper, whom he had seen alive the day before, was dead. Indians had killed him and driven off all the horses. Pony Bob had no choice but to ride on. He stopped just long enough to give his tired horse some water.

Pony Bob headed for Sand Springs, the next station. It was growing dark and his horse was jumpy. "The stillness of the night and the howling of wolves and coyotes sent cold chills through me," he later recalled.

He finally arrived at Sand Springs and told the stock tender what had happened. He said it was too dangerous for the man to stay there alone. The man agreed to leave with Pony Bob.

Pony Bob finally arrived back at Bucklands Station just three hours behind schedule. In thirty-six hours, he had ridden 380 miles. It was the longest ride of any Pony Express rider on record. The station keeper who had promised him a bonus raised it from fifty dollars to one hundred dollars. He felt Pony Bob had earned every penny of it.

The stock tender from Sand Springs owed his life to Pony Bob. The very next morning, Indians attacked his station and burned it to the ground.

Pony Bob hadn't run into any Indians on his record-breaking ride. But his luck didn't last. Soon after, he rode into a war party of thirty Paiutes. They were blocking the trail in front of him. Instead of turning his horse around and fleeing, Pony Bob held his ground. He pulled out his Colt revolver and rode directly toward the Indians. To his amazement, their leader cried out his admiration at such bravery. He told the others to let the rider pass.

Changing Times

In May 1860, nine hundred U.S. soldiers arrived in Utah to fight the Paiutes. Being outnumbered, the Indians fled north. The Paiute War came to an end.

The Paiute War had dealt a heavy blow to the Pony Express. The company had to stop mail delivery for six weeks during the war. It lost thousands of dollars in property damage and income.

In March 1861, Abraham Lincoln was sworn in as the new president of the United States.

The company had to choose a rider to carry President Lincoln's inaugural address through Nevada to California. There was no question about who would get this important assignment—Pony Bob. Lincoln's speech reached Sacramento from St. Joseph in record time—seven days and seventeen hours.

Pony Bob was proud to carry President Lincoln's inaugural address to California.

Pony Bob (back row, left) was one of the Pony Express's most dedicated riders. He gained the respect of others for his strong work ethic, including Alexander Majors (seated, center) and Buffalo Bill (seated, right).

When the Pony Express ended, Pony Bob continued to ride on his old route for Wells, Fargo, and Company. He later worked as a deputy U.S. Marshal in Salt Lake City.

Pony Bob didn't much like being a lawman. He spent his last years working at the Hotel Congress in Chicago. There, he entertained hotel guests with stories of his youthful adventures as a Pony Express rider.

7

More Dangers on the Trail

Several dangers that Pony Express riders faced on the trail are clear from the stories told thus far. However, these weren't the only dangers on the trail. Riders also had to face wolves, blizzards, overflowing rivers, and quicksand. With all of these dangers and the long rides, lack of sleep posed a real danger, too.

Wolves

A man named William Campbell was riding on his route one night when he came upon a large pack of wolves. The wolves were devouring a dead animal. Whatever animal it was, it didn't satisfy the wolves' hunger. When they saw Campbell ride by on his pony, they wanted to kill and eat the pony, too. The wolves took chase.

Pony Express riders were given two revolvers, a rifle, and a Bowie knife in case they had to defend themselves. Unfortunately, Campbell wasn't carrying any of his weapons at the time. Many riders didn't carry weapons because the weapons weighed them down.

The wolves traveled in packs, hunting their prey together.

All Campbell had was the horn he used to signal the station keeper of his arrival. As the wolves were gaining on him, Campbell blew the horn. The loud blast of noise frightened the wolves. They fell back. After a while, their courage returned and they drew nearer. Campbell blew his horn again. Again, they fell back. He kept this up until he had reached the station and safety.

Blizzards

Campbell and other riders were at times caught in blizzards. The wind and snow were so blinding during one blizzard that Campbell couldn't tell where the trail was. Snow had piled up to six feet in some places.

Campbell knew that losing his way in the snowstorm might cause both him and his horse to die. Campbell stayed calm. He noticed the tops of the tall weeds along either side of the trail. By following the weeds, he was able to stay on the trail. When night fell, the instincts of his horse returned them safely to the station.

After his time with the Pony Express, Campbell moved to Nebraska City, Nebraska. He became one of the town's leading citizens. He was even elected to the state Senate. William Campbell died at age ninety in 1932, one of the last surviving Pony Express riders.

Overflowing Rivers and Quicksand

Melting snow could be as dangerous as falling snow for Pony Express riders. In the spring, melting snow ran down mountains and turned gentle streams and rivers into dangerous waterways.

One Pony Express rider was crossing the Platte River when the swift current carried him and his horse downstream. Suddenly, the horse found itself sinking into a bed of quicksand on the river bottom. The more the poor animal struggled, the deeper it sank into the quicksand. The rider jumped off the helpless horse, grabbed the mochila, and climbed to the shore.

The more the horse struggled, the deeper it sank into the deadly quicksand.

A crowd had gathered there. One man offered the rider his horse. The grateful Pony Express rider thanked the man. Then he took off on the horse without another word. The crowd then rushed to the river to rescue the other horse from the quicksand.

Lack of Sleep

Even the most skilled rider on the trail was often unable to overcome the lack of sleep. Riding could become quite boring, especially on the flatlands of Kansas and Nebraska. Many a rider dozed off on his horse under these conditions, but the alert animal kept moving. One time, two sleeping Pony Express riders going in opposite directions passed each other and didn't even know it!

Sometimes an unlucky rider would slip right out of the saddle as he slept. Then, he would suddenly wake up and find himself on the cold ground in the middle of nowhere. It might take him hours to walk to the next station. But when he got there, he would always find that his faithful horse had arrived before him with the mail.

CHAPTER

8

The End of the Trail

The Pony Express could survive Indians and outlaws. It could survive wild animals and bad weather. But it could not survive a new invention called the telegraph.

American inventor Samuel F. B. Morse developed the telegraph. Morse found a way to send electrical impulses across wires by using a code. The Morse Code's dots, dashes, and spaces could be translated into letters to form words.

In May 1844, Morse sent a four-word message over a telegraph line between Washington, D.C., and Baltimore, Maryland. Success!

After years of work, the telegraph lines reached all the way to Salt Lake City, Utah. The work was completed on October 24, 1861. At that time, it took the Pony Express ten days to get a message from St. Joseph to Sacramento. The same message could now be sent across telegraph lines in about ten minutes.

Morse Code

A • —	J • — — —	S • • •
B — • • •	K — • —	T —
C — • — •	L • — • •	U • • —
D — • •	M — —	V • • • —
E •	N — •	W • — —
F • • — •	O — — —	X — • • —
G — — •	P • — — •	Y — • — —
H • • • •	Q — — • —	Z — — • •
I • •	R • — •	

1 • — — — —	Period • — • — • —
2 • • — — —	Comma — — • • — —
3 • • • — —	
4 • • • • —	
5 • • • • •	
6 — • • • •	
7 — — • • •	
8 — — — • •	
9 — — — — •	
0 — — — — —	

Samuel F. B. Morse's invention was the beginning of a new era in communication.

This Pony Express rider salutes the telegraph lines that will soon replace him.

Goodbye, Pony Express

The Pony Express was no longer needed. Two days after the lines were completed, the Pony Express went out of business. It had lasted eighteen months.

The Pony Express had been a financial disaster. Russell, Majors, and Waddell lost more than five hundred thousand dollars. The government contract that Russell hoped for never came. He and his partners soon went bankrupt. Both Russell and Waddell died penniless. Alexander Majors did somewhat better. Years later, he wrote a book about his life in the West.

This trail marker honoring the Pony Express and its founders was made during the Pony Express's one hundredth birthday.

What happened to the Pony Express riders? Some continued to work as riders for other businesses. Others became scouts for the U.S. Army in the West. William F. Cody (Buffalo Bill) was one of these. Still others signed up to fight in the Civil War, which began in April 1861. Pony rider Johnny Fry was killed in battle fighting for the Union.

Few Pony Express workers did as well as Sam Gilson. Gilson had sold horses to the Pony Express. Years later, he discovered a coal-like mineral called *asphaltum* in Utah. He found that asphaltum could be used as a building material. Asphaltum made Sam Gilson rich. Its name was even changed to "Gilsonite" in his honor.

Still, a Success Story

Despite the loss of money, the Pony Express was a great success in many ways. In 308 complete runs, riders covered a distance equal to going around the earth more than thirty times! They delivered a total of 34,753 letters. Only one mochila was lost in those 308 runs. Only one rider was killed when Indians attacked him.

This letter was delivered by the Pony Express. Note the cancellation marks on it.

The Pony Express was important for other reasons, too. Many people in the North (the Union) were afraid that California would join the South (the Confederacy) in the Civil War. If it did, California's gold could be used to help the Southern cause.

The Pony Express kept Californians up-to-date on the war's progress. It delivered the inspiring words of President Lincoln. Many Californians identified closely with the North and its cause. The news they received from the Pony Express supported their beliefs. This was an important factor in keeping California and its gold in the Union.

The Pony Express was one of the most exciting chapters in the story of the West. That story has been retold in books, paintings, and movies. The courage and skill of the riders of the Pony Express continue to inspire Americans today.

How Americans felt about the Pony Express was perhaps best put by one California newspaper writer. "A fast and faithful friend has the Pony [Express] been to our far-off state," he wrote. "Goodbye, Pony!....You have served us well."

This statue of a Pony Express rider in Salt Lake City, Utah, was completed in 1998.

Index